GALE
CENGAGE Learning

Novels for Students, Volume 12

Staff

Editor: Elizabeth Thomason.

Contributing Editors: Reginald Carlton, Anne Marie Hacht, Michael L. LaBlanc, Ira Mark Milne, Jennifer Smith.

Managing Editor, Content: Dwayne D. Hayes.

Managing Editor, Product: David Galens.

Publisher, Literature Product: Mark Scott.

Literature Content Capture: Joyce Nakamura, *Managing Editor*. Sara Constantakis, *Editor*.

Research: Victoria B. Cariappa, *Research Manager*. Cheryl Warnock, *Research Specialist*. Tamara Nott, Tracie A. Richardson, *Research Associates*. Nicodemus Ford, Sarah Genik, Timothy Lehnerer, Ron Morelli, *Research Assistants*.

Permissions: Maria Franklin, *Permissions Manager*.

Jacqueline Jones, Julie Juengling, *Permissions Assistants*.

Manufacturing: Mary Beth Trimper, *Manager, Composition and Electronic Prepress*. Evi Seoud, *Assistant Manager, Composition Purchasing and Electronic Prepress*. Stacy Melson, *Buyer*.

Imaging and Multimedia Content Team: Barbara Yarrow, *Manager*. Randy Bassett, *Imaging Supervisor*. Robert Duncan, Dan Newell, *Imaging Specialists*. Pamela A. Reed, *Imaging Coordinator*. Leitha Etheridge-Sims, Mary Grimes, David G. Oblender, *Image Catalogers*. Robyn V. Young, *Project Manager*. Dean Dauphinais, *Senior Image Editor*. Kelly A. Quin, *Image Editor*.

Product Design Team: Kenn Zorn, *Product Design Manager*. Pamela A. E. Galbreath, *Senior Art Director*. Michael Logusz, *Graphic Artist*.

Copyright Notice

individual does not imply endorsement of the editors or publisher. Errors brought to the attention of the publisher and verified to the satisfaction of the publisher will be corrected in future editions.

This publication is a creative work fully protected by all applicable copyright laws, as well as by misappropriation, trade secret, unfair competition, and other applicable laws. The authors and editors of this work have added value to the underlying factual material herein through one or more of the following: unique and original selection, coordination, expression, arrangement, and classification of the information. All rights to this publication will be vigorously defended.

Little Women

Louisa May Alcott 1868

Introduction

Without a doubt, *Little Women* remains Louisa May Alcott's best-known work. Its charm and innocence continue to engage readers, despite the fact that the social and familial reality depicted is very different from contemporary domestic life. Jo March is regarded as one of the most complete, self-possessed, and best-loved characters in children's literature. In fact, many boys find that they can relate to her almost as easily as girls can. While some present-day readers find Jo and her sisters too good to be realistic, according to the standards of Alcott's society, the March girls are flawed and vulnerable. The author dared to give her characters faults such as selfishness, vanity, temper, and bash-fulness—qualities never seen before in such young characters.

Alcott wrote the book for girls with the sole aim of making money with its publication. After part one was published as a complete work, readers demanded to know more about the fates of the Marches. Alcott wrote *Good Wives* which is now published with part one as a complete work. Although the author wrote the books reluctantly, she earned the money she sought and found that her subsequent titles of all kinds were widely read. She never imagined, however, that *Little Women* would enchant generations of readers and become a classic of children's fiction. Critics often note that the book's particular appeal lies in its illustration of a uniquely American household and its individual members. Almost any reader can identify with at least one of the four girls. Readers are also drawn into the story by the colorful minor characters, the development of the March girls, and the attention to detail. The intricacies of education, housework, speech patterns, and manners are depicted with remarkable clarity, which better enables modern readers to envision and understand the world of the Marches.

Author Biography

Born on November 29, 1832, in Germantown, Pennsylvania, Louisa May Alcott is best remembered for her books about the March family, especially her children's masterpiece, *Little Women*. From the 1840s into the late 1860s, Alcott (under the pseudonyms A. M. Barnard and Flora Fairchild) also wrote sensational novels and thrillers for adults, most of which are no longer in print. Ironically, Alcott preferred her adult novels to the children's novels that account for her lasting fame.

The Alcotts lived in Concord, Massachusetts, with friends and neighbors such as Ralph Waldo Emerson, Henry David Thoreau, and Nathaniel Hawthorne. Alcott's youth was shaped by both the philosophical climate and the poverty in which she lived. Bronson Alcott, Louisa's father, was a transcendentalist thinker and writer who refused to take work that was not related to education or philosophy. (Transcendentalism is a philosophy that holds that there is an ideal spiritual reality beyond material reality.) Unemployed, he committed to educating his four daughters, Anna (Meg in *Little Women*), Louisa (Jo), Elizabeth (Beth), and May (Amy). A radical pioneer in education, his experiments yielded an erratic but thorough education for his daughters. In 1843, he initiated a largescale experiment known as Fruitlands, an effort to create a utopian society. Within a year, it failed, and while Alcott seemed flippant about the failure, this experience showed that Bronson could not be relied upon to support the family. Responsibility fell on Alcott's mother, Abba, who came from a respected Boston family. For thirty years, she did the housework and supported the family as a social worker.

Recognizing their daughter's talent, Bronson and Abba placed heavy expectations on her. She was a creative, difficult, and willful girl who was both moody and loyal. As a child, Alcott doted on Emerson and accompanied Thoreau on nature walks in the area of Walden Pond. Although surrounded by transcendentalists, she eventually rejected the philosophy as too abstract, using fiction to give voice to her objections. Still, Alcott's writing demonstrates her acceptance of the transcendentalist emphasis on self-reliance and independence.

Little Women contains many autobiographical elements, and critics are quick to note that the stormy character Jo is modeled after Alcott herself. This novel, along with the seven others featuring the March family, is cherished for its cheerful depiction of domestic life, its wholesomeness, and its ability to teach life lessons without the preachy quality found in other children's novels.

Alcott began *Little Women* in 1868, after the Civil War, in which she had served as a nurse during the winter of 1862–1863. She completed part one in only six weeks, and did not revise it as she was in the habit of doing for her adult fiction. It was published as a complete novel. When her public demanded to know more about the Marches, she wrote part two the following year. The novel alludes to the war, but does not include lengthy passages about its disastrous effects on American families and the country as a whole. Her contemporaries, after all, did not need such explanations. In her introduction to the novel, Ann Douglas observes, "*Little Women*, like its avowed model, *Pilgrim's Progress*, is in part an allegory. Alcott was writing about a house in conflict but not divided, a family that offered an analogy and possibly a corrective to America."

By the time *Little Women* was published, Alcott had already become fiercely private. She dreaded interacting with her readers, preferring instead to stay home with her family. Her brief stint as a nurse left her health permanently weakened, a condition that got worse with age. She never married, and, as she grew older, she took very seriously her role as the provider and caretaker of her family. In the end, she was unhappy and unsatisfied with her life. She believed, as do many critics, that her talent was greater than the children's books for which she is so fondly remembered. Alcott died on March 6, 1888, in Boston.

Plot Summary

Part One, Chapters 1-12

The March girls—Meg, 17, Jo, 16, Beth, 14, and Amy, 12—bemoan the fact that Christmas will be lacking because their poverty prevents them from having gifts and their father is away in the Civil War. Resolving to be better people, they decide to play Pilgrim's Progress, an ongoing make-believe in which they follow the allegorical travels of Christian in John Bunyan's *Pilgrim's Progress*. On Christmas day, the girls take their breakfast to the Hummels, a needy family nearby. Later, they discover that their wealthy neighbor Mr. Laurence has rewarded their kindness with flowers and treats.

Jo and Meg attend a dance at a neighbor's house, and while Meg dances, Jo hides behind a curtain. She finds Mr. Laurence's grandson, Theodore ("Laurie"), also hiding. They become quick friends, and when Meg twists her ankle, Laurie gives the girls a ride home.

With the holidays over, the girls resume their routines. Meg is a governess, Jo is the companion of feisty Aunt March (Mr. March's aunt), Beth studies at home, and Amy goes to school. Each girl has an artistic talent: Beth loves music, Jo writes stories and plays, Meg acts in Jo's plays, and Amy draws and sculpts clay.

The girls readily befriend Laurie and his grandfather and visit their luxurious house, enjoying the conservatory, the library, and the piano. The March girls even allow Laurie into their secret club. They set up a post office between the houses in which they can exchange letters, books, flowers, and packages.

Amy buys pickled limes for her friends at school, as this is the fashionable thing to do. When the teacher, who has forbidden students to bring limes to school, catches her with them, she is scolded, her hands are swatted, and she is made to stand in front of the class until recess. Humiliated, she goes home, where Mrs. March tells her she can study at home with Beth rather than return to school.

In a tantrum because Jo and Meg will not let her accompany them to the theater with Laurie, Amy burns the book Jo has been writing. Jo is furious and unforgiving until Amy follows her to ice skate with Laurie and falls through the ice because Jo did not caution her. Jo is ashamed and forgives her sister while resolving to control her anger.

Meg visits her wealthy friend, Annie Moffat, and feels uncomfortable in her shabby clothes. Her friends dress her up for a dance and she soon feels foolish for being treated like a doll.

While Aunt March and Meg's employers are away, the girls say how much they would like to do nothing but play. To teach them a lesson, Marmee agrees to free them of all chores for one week. One disaster after another ensues, and the girls learn the value of work.

Laurie hosts a picnic across the river and invites the girls to join him and his friends. They eat, talk, and play games, and it becomes apparent that Mr. Brooke, Laurie's tutor, has eyes for Meg.

Part One, Chapters 13-23

Jo submits stories to a local newspaper, and the family is ecstatic when they are published. Marmee receives a telegram with the news that her husband is ill and she should come right away. Mr. Laurence sends Mr. Brooke to accompany her on the trip, and the girls worry and promise to write often. Because Marmee is faced with borrowing money, Jo sells her beautiful hair for twenty-five dollars. While Marmee is away, Beth tries to get the other girls to visit the Hummels. When Beth contracts scarlet fever from the sick Hummel baby, the other March girls are ashamed of their selfishness. To protect her from the disease, Amy is sent to live with Aunt March until Beth recovers, and the old woman is quite taken with the young girl. When Beth's condition worsens, they send for Marmee, but the fever breaks just before she arrives. All are relieved and happy to be reunited.

Jo tells Marmee that Mr. Brooke is in love with Meg. Marmee explains that on the trip, Mr. Brooke told her and Mr. March that he loved Meg and hoped to marry her. They said he could make plans, but that Meg was too young to be engaged. When Laurie suspects that Jo knows something about the couple that she will not tell, he plays a cruel joke. He sends Meg letters signed with Mr. Brooke's name. When he is caught, he is regretful and Meg is embarrassed.

Christmas arrives again and Laurie surprises the Marches by bringing Mr. March home.

Mr. Brooke visits Meg and tells her that he loves her and hopes she can learn to feel the same way. Playing games, she acts very cruelly toward him until Aunt March interrupts and Mr. Brooke leaves. Aunt March tells Meg that Meg can do better than Mr. Brooke, and that if she marries him, she will be out of her aunt's will. Indignant, Meg says she can marry whomever she pleases and that Mr. Brooke is a fine man. Aunt March leaves, and Mr. Brooke returns, having overheard everything. The couple agrees to marry, although they will have to wait three years for Meg to grow older and Mr. Brooke to make living arrangements.

Part Two, Chapters 24-35

Three years have passed, and Meg prepares for her wedding. The war is over, and Mr. March is a minister. Aunt March has released Jo from her duty and instead employs Amy to be her companion, paying her with expensive art lessons. Beth is still a homebody, and her health is frail since her fever. Jo sells stories and enjoys life as a writer, feeling quite independent. She enters a contest and wins $100, and the family is very impressed with the sensational story. Papa commends his daughter, adding that he thinks she can do even better. When Jo finishes her novel, she submits it for publication but is advised that it requires major revisions. Torn between her commitment to the novel as it is and wanting to get it published, she decides to go ahead and "chop it up." Reviews are mixed, and Jo regrets her compromise, but she learns about the rigors and trials of being a novelist.

Resigned to the upcoming marriage, Aunt March's stance has softened, and she purchases beautiful linens for the couple's new home. Laurie tells Jo she will be the next to marry, but she responds that she has no interest in such things. On the day of the wedding, family and a few friends gather at the March home for a lovely, simple wedding.

Meg soon finds that married life is satisfying, if not a fairy tale. She has twins, a boy and a girl named Demi and Daisy.

Aunt Carrol plans a trip to Europe, and Aunt March pays for Amy to go along so she can study art. Jo decides to go to New York, where she will teach at a boarding house. There, she meets Professor Bhaer, a charming, poor, German man. When Jo returns home in the summer, Laurie tells her he loves her and wants to marry her. She turns down his proposal, which devastates him. A few weeks later, Mr. Laurence leaves for Europe and Laurie decides to accompany him.

Part Two, Chapters 36-47

Beth's health has been declining steadily over the years, and now she dies peacefully.

In Europe, Laurie makes a last effort to change Jo's mind by correspondence. When she again declines, he begins to correspond with Amy, whom he has seen in his travels. The news of Beth's death sends Laurie to find Amy at once, and romance blooms.

Amy and Laurie return from Europe married, and Jo is surprised but delighted for the union of her little sister and best friend. Professor Bhaer becomes a regular visitor to the March home. One day, he tells Jo he loves her and she kisses him. Aunt March has died and left a country home, Plumfield, to Jo. When she and Bhaer marry, they open a boys' school there.

The family has expanded with husbands and children, but the girls find it as happy as when it was just the four of them, Marmee, and Papa.

Professor Friedrich ("Fritz") Bhaer

On her trip to New York, Jo meets Professor Bhaer, a German man with a thick accent. He is a stout, educated, older man who takes care of his two orphaned nephews, Franz and Emil. Because he is a bachelor, he undertakes such domestic tasks as cleaning and darning his own socks.

When Jo returns home, Bhaer makes frequent visits, and he and Jo eventually marry. He encourages her to keep writing, but to challenge her talent by writing good fiction rather than the sensationalistic pieces she usually writes. He and Jo open a boys' school at Plumfield.

Mr. John Brooke

Mr. Brooke is Laurie's tutor. As he gets to know Meg, he falls in love with her. In accordance with her parents' request, he waits to marrry Meg until she turns twenty. This period gives him an opportunity to estabish himself and buy a house. Although Mr. Laurence offers to help Mr. Brooke, the young man refuses, preferring to make his own way without incurring any debt.

Mr. Brooke takes a job as a clerk and earns a

modest living for himself and his new bride.

Hannah

Hannah is the March family's housekeeper. She is colorful and energetic, and she loves the family dearly. She has been with the family since Mr. and Mrs. March married, and she gave Mrs. March her first cooking lessons.

Mr. Laurence

Mr. Laurence is Laurie's grandfather. Until the March sisters meet him, they imagine him to be a daunting man who is distant and stern. Once they get to know him, however, they find him to be generous and warm. He takes a special liking to Jo for her audacity, and he feels special warmth toward Beth.

Theodore Laurence

See Laurie

Laurie

Laurie is the next-door neighbor and is the same age as Jo, his best friend. Although Laurie is wealthy, the economic difference between himself and the Marches does not factor into their relationships. Laurie is instructed at home by a tutor, Mr. Brooke, and later attends college. Laurie is a handsome, friendly, intelligent, witty, and dashing young man who delights in the capers of his neighbors.

Laurie lives with his grandfather, Mr. Laurence, because both of his parents have died. Mr. Laurence was very displeased when his son married Laurie's mother, an Italian woman who was accomplished in music. Living with only his grandfather, Laurie is lonely and therefore treasures his friendships with the March girls and Marmee.

After graduating from college, Laurie proposes to Jo, who rejects him. Devastated, he accompanies his grandfather to Europe, where he and Amy fall in love and marry.

Media Adaptations

- *Little Women* has been adapted for the screen on numerous occasions. The first was a silent movie produced by G. B. Samuelson in

1917. In 1918, William A. Brady Picture Plays produced another silent version, adapted by Anne Maxwell. One of the best-known adaptations was produced in 1933 by RKO Radio Pictures, adapted for film by Sarah Y. Mason and Victor Heerman, starring Katharine Hepburn as Jo. In 1949, an adaptation by Mason, Heerman, and Andrew Solt was produced by MGM, starring June Allyson as Jo, Elizabeth Taylor as Amy, Janet Leigh as Meg, and Peter Lawford as Laurie. In 1994, Columbia Pictures produced a film adaptation by Robin Swicord, starring Winona Ryder as Jo, Kirsten Dunst as Amy, Claire Danes as Beth, Eric Stoltz as Mr. Brooke, and Susan Sarandon as Marmee.

- *Little Women* was adapted for television in 1958 in a production by CBS Television. Another television production was released in 1970, directed by Paddy Russell. In 1978, an adaptation for television by Susan Clauser was produced by Universal TV, starring Meredith Baxter as Meg, Susan Dey as Jo, Eve Plumb as Beth, Greer Garson as Aunt March, and William Shatner as Professor Bhaer.

- Numerous audio adaptations have been made for listeners to enjoy the story on tape. These include releases by Books in Motion, 1982; Audio Book Contractors, 1987; Harper Audio, 1991; DH Audio, 1992; Dove Entertainment, 1995; Soundelux Audio Publishing, 1995; Sterling Audio Books, 1995; Penguin, 1996; Black-stone Audio Books, 1997; Random House Audio Books, 1997; Trafalgar Square, 1997; Bantam Books, 1998; Books on Tape, 1998; Brilliance Audio, 1998; Monterey Soundworks, 1998; and Naxos Audio Books, 2000.

Amy March

Amy is the youngest of the March girls and is twelve at the beginning of the novel. She is spoiled and throws tantrums, and her family strives to correct her behavior before she gets older. Like Meg, Amy loves luxuries and takes an interest in her appearance that is unusual for someone so young. She is also concerned with behaving properly and being popular among her peers. Her pride is her beautiful hair, which falls into golden ringlets. Amy is the artist of the family and spends time drawing and sculpting animals out of clay.

When Beth becomes ill, Amy is sent to stay

with Aunt March, who likes the little girl very much. Aunt March releases Jo from her duty as a companion and instead employs Amy, for whom she provides expensive art lessons. Amy travels with another family member to Europe (at Aunt March's expense). While Amy is in Europe, Beth dies and Laurie (also traveling in Europe) finds Amy to comfort her. The two fall in love and marry.

Amy's marriage is comfortable because she marries a man she cares for who happens to be wealthy. Unlike the other sisters, Amy never has to worry about work and has all the fine things she always desired.

Aunt March

Mr. March's aunt, Aunt March is a wealthy widow whose views represent the typical opinions of the time. She believes that Meg, with her beauty, should set her sights on marrying a rich man to provide for her and her family. When Meg considers Mr. Brooke's offer of marriage, Aunt March threatens Meg, saying that if she marries him, she will never get any of Aunt March's money. However, she eventually softens and makes a lovely gift of linens for the couple.

In the beginning of the story, Aunt March pays Jo to be her companion but later hires Amy instead. She is taken with Amy's lively, yet prim nature and hopes to mold her.

When Aunt March dies, she leaves her country home, called Plumfield, to Jo.

Beth March

Beth is the second youngest of the March girls. She is fourteen as the story opens, and she is painfully shy and withdrawn. Although she loves her family and is comfortable with them, she is fearful of strangers and relies on Jo to watch over her. Too shy to attend public school, she studies at home. Beth never makes plans for the future and never talks about having any dreams; she seems perfectly content with her life as it is and expects it to stay the same.

Beth's disposition is sweet, selfless, and warm. She never asks for anything for herself and seeks only to make those around her happy. Her talent is for music, and she makes do on an old wornout keyboard until Mr. Laurence allows her to play the beautiful piano at his house. She and Mr. Laurence develop a grandfather-granddaughter relationship that fulfills them both.

While caring for a poor family, Beth contracts scarlet fever and becomes extremely ill. Her fever breaks before it claims her life, but her health is permanently compromised by the ordeal. Years later, her health finally gives out, and Beth dies as a young woman.

Josephine March

The second eldest of the four March sisters, Jo is independent, tempestuous, vivacious, clever, and self-confident. She struggles throughout the story to learn to control her temper and her tendency to hold a grudge. She is a tomboy who is more interested in reading and playing games than in primping or gossiping with girls her age. She is sixteen when the story opens, and she has no desire to get married, preferring the happy and satisfying life she enjoys with her family. In fact, when Meg prepares for marriage, Jo is very upset at the prospect of the family breaking up. No longer in school, Jo is the paid companion of Aunt March, a duty she fulfills out of obligation.

Jo has a special relationship with Beth, the next youngest sister. While all of the girls look to Marmee for guidance and advice, Jo watches over Beth and provides additional sisterly support. Jo's relationship with Beth reveals a soft, maternal side of Jo that is rarely seen.

Besides reading, Jo loves to write plays and short stories. The girls enjoy performing Jo's plays, in which she always plays the men's roles. After having two of her stories accepted for publication by a local newspaper, Jo takes her writing more seriously, falling into whirlwind "fits" of writing. Writing brings her success and allows her to earn money doing something she loves. As she observes other young women, Jo is proud of herself because she is able to earn her own money and feel independent. Jo writes a novel, which is accepted for publication only after substantial revision. Jo agrees to the overhaul because she is anxious to get the book published.

Jo's best friend is the wealthy young man next

door, Laurie. Jo appeals to him because he can relate to her almost as if she were a boy. Their friendship is characterized by equality, love of books, and a sense of adventure. After graduating from college, Laurie proposes to Jo, but she rejects his proposal, despite knowing that their friendship will be forever changed. Most critics agree that she turns him down because he will never take seriously her career as a writer and because she loves him in a sisterly way, not as a lover. When Laurie marries Amy, Jo is genuinely happy for them. Eventually, Jo marries Professor Bhaer, an older man who is poor, educated, and supportive of her career. Together, they start a school for boys at Plumfield and later have two boys of their own.

Marmee March

Marmee is the girls' mother. She is a strong, confident, reliable woman who provides moral instruction, guidance, and support for her daughters at every stage of their lives. While her husband is away at war, Marmee must care for the house and the four girls on her own. She never appears to struggle, however. She makes certain demands on the girls so that they will learn valuable lessons about life.

Marmee encourages her girls to think for themselves and to pursue true happiness, which, she believes, does not necessarily come from having money. If her daughters never marry, Marmee will be satisfied as long as they are wise, respectable, and accomplished women. She tells Meg that the secret to a good marriage is mutual understanding. She and Mr. March each have their gender-specific duties, but they cooperate with each other and have their own identities.

Meg March

Meg is the eldest of the four girls. Seventeen as the book opens, she is drawn to domestic affairs and feels rewarded when she is able to please those around her. Being old enough to remember times before her family lost its money, she longs for many of the luxuries she can no longer enjoy. She works as a governess for the Kings, who have two children.

Meg has a special relationship with Amy, and acts as her advisor and protector. Meg and Amy have some superficial qualities in common, such as vanity and love of finery, but Meg's temperament is much gentler than Amy's is.

Meg is regarded as beautiful and, as a result, she struggles with her own vanity. She adores wearing fine dresses and having nice things, but such items remain out of reach. When Laurie's tutor, Mr. Brooke, proposes to her, she accepts despite the fact that he is a poor clerk. She sees that he is a good and honest man, and overcomes her disappointment that they are not a well-to-do couple.

Meg delights in domestic activities such as cooking, sewing, and keeping the house in order.

Her marriage to Mr. Brooke is happy, but she has difficulty with the initial transition because she wants so badly to be the perfect wife to him. They have twins, a boy named Demi and a girl named Daisy. Meg and Mr. Brooke's gender roles are traditional—he works and disciplines the children, and she does all household work.

Mr. March

The March girls' father, "Papa" (or "Father"), is away serving as a chaplain in the Civil War. He writes loving letters home to his family, and when he is stricken with illness, Marmee leaves the girls to take care of him.

After the war, Mr. March returns and takes a position as a minister in a local church. His days are filled with ministering to his parishioners and interacting with an interesting and diverse group of people. Just as the sisters are based on Alcott's own sisters, Mr. March is based on Alcott's father. Although Mr. March is an important figure in the family's life, he is seen very little in the action of the novel.

Annie Moffat

A wealthy friend of Meg's, Annie invites Meg to stay with her for two weeks, and they dress up for a dance.

Teddy

See Laurie

Themes

Gender Roles

Little Women challenged assumptions about women in nineteenth-century America. Marmee tells her daughters that they should not feel obligated to find husbands, but should seek fulfillment on their own. In chapter 9, she tells Meg and Jo:

> My dear girls, I *am* ambitious for you, but not to have you make a dash in the world—marry rich men merely because they are rich, or have splendid houses, which are not homes because love is wanting…. [B]etter be happy old maids than unhappy wives, or unmaidenly girls, running about to have husbands…. Leave these things to time; make this home happy, so that you may be fit for homes of your own, if they are offered you, and contented here if they are not.

Through her example, Marmee shows that a home can be run successfully without a man supporting it, as hers is while Mr. March is away at war. While many women, like Aunt March, expected young women to pursue wealthy men, Marmee sees the value of marriage differently.

Jo is fascinating as a study of female independence in early American society. She is a tomboy who is scolded by her sisters for whistling, using slang, and behaving in "unmaidenly" ways. In chapter 1, Jo tells Meg:

> I hate to think I've got to grow up, and be Miss March, and wear long gowns, and look as prim as a China aster! It's bad enough to be a girl, anyway, when I like boys' games and work and manners! I can't get over my disappointment in not being a boy; and it's worse than ever now, for I'm dying to go and fight with Papa, and I can only stay at home and knit, like a poky old woman!

Jo is brash, outspoken, lively, and clever. She proclaims, "I am not afraid of anything," voicing an attitude altogether different from that of the stereotypical prim and proper young lady. As she matures, she takes more care with her appearance and adopts more ladylike mannerisms, but she does not sacrifice the sense that she is equal to any man.

Adolescence and Identity

Although Meg, Jo, Beth, and Amy grow up in the same household, they develop very distinct identities. Marmee encourages them to be confident in themselves and to mature in wisdom and self-knowledge. Adolescence is a difficult period for anyone, so the girls' struggles are universal.

Throughout the novel, the girls' basic identities remain consistent, but as they grow up, they come to understand their faults and work to improve themselves.

Meg's identity is anchored in pleasing her family, be it her mother and sisters or her husband. She is domestic and thrives on homemaking. Jo is stormy and independent, but eventually learns to control her temper. Even as an adult, the selfreliance she values is important in her decision-making. Jo is an unconventional person, so it is no surprise that she ultimately lives an unconventional life. Beth is harmonious and selfless. Were it not for her untimely death, she would likely have continued to grow as a warm and giving person who stays close to home. As the youngest, Amy is somewhat spoiled and acquires a taste for the finer things. This identity is fed by her marriage to Laurie, a wealthy husband who will dote on her and give her everything she desires.

Topics for Further Study

- Imagine you are assigned to create a soundtrack for *Little Women*. Think about each of the four March girls, Laurie, and Marmee. Choose a song or musical composition that best reflects each character's personality, dreams, and emotional landscape. What are the songs that you choose?

- Research birth-order theories and consider how the dynamics among the sisters support or refute such theories. Report on your findings.

- Although modern wars have important roles for women, the Civil War was much more of a man's war. See what you can learn about women during the time of the Civil War. In what ways did they contribute to the war effort both on the front (in hospitals, for example) and at home?

- Examine the lives of other prominent American women writers to see if there are parallels between their life experiences and Louisa May Alcott's. Do you find that they are vastly different, or that there are significant similarities? Also, did most women use their given names, or did they take pseudonyms, perhaps even male pseudonyms (such as British author George Eliot)? How do you account for the decision to reveal female gender (or not) as a writer in the nineteenth century?

Wealth and Poverty

The Marches are poor, although not so poor that they cannot help others. There is never any danger of the March family starving or losing their home, but they all know that they have little money to spare and must economize. Alcott teaches that everyone, even those who have little, has something to offer the world. Marmee and Beth's dedication to the poor German family, the Hummels, is evidence that for all their complaints, the Marches are quite fortunate. Laurie, who comes from a wealthy family. lives right next door to the Marches, and the contrast between the two houses is striking. In chapter 5, Alcott writes, "A low hedge parted the two estates. On one side was an old, brown house, looking rather bare and shabby.... On the other side was a stately stone mansion, plainly betokening every sort of comfort and luxury."

The economic inequality between the families, however, has no effect on their relationships. The girls enjoy visiting the Laurences' home to browse the library, admire the art, or stroll among the flowers in the conservatory. Yet there is no bitterness or deep envy. In fact, when the Laurences offer gifts, the Marches feel compelled to return the kindness, and do so without feeling that their offerings are any less valued. The affection between the families neutralizes economic differences that would taint weaker relationships.

Alcott shows, too, that the Marches are rich in ways that the Laurences are not. The Marches, after all, have a house full of lively girls who love one another and have fun together. There is a mother and a father, neither of which Laurie has, and a strong family foundation. Laurie admits to Jo that he watches the activities of the March house, and she understands his loneliness. Once they are friends, the girls make an effort to include Laurie in their fun, including initiating him into their secret club. By presenting the disparities between the two families as she does, Alcott clearly shows her young readers that there are many kinds of wealth and poverty.

The "Good Match"

Although Aunt March attempts to exert her influence to see that Meg is married to an appropriately rich young man, Marmee knows better. Mr. Brooke accompanies Marmee to visit her sick husband and is forthright about his feelings for Meg. Marmee and Mr. March see that he is an honorable man who is a good match for their daughter. Still, the decision is Meg's—if she could not love Mr. Brooke, her parents would in no way force the union. This difference of opinion about what constitutes a "good match" shows the social views of the time, as expressed by Aunt March, in contrast to Alcott's own views, as expressed by Marmee.

Readers are often surprised and disappointed that Jo rejects Laurie's proposal of marriage. They are great friends, and he is charming, handsome, and passionate. Jo knows, however, that Laurie regards her writing as just another "lark" and would never fully support her efforts to make a career of writing. Further, it is clear that Jo's feelings for Laurie are friendly, even sisterly, and she cannot love him romantically. Her decision not to marry him is respectful of herself and of Laurie, as she wants him to have a wife who will love him as a wife should. By marrying Professor Bhaer, Jo can be herself, an independent woman who enjoys writing and teaching. Bhaer does not discourage her writing, but encourages her to try to do better than the sensational stories that come so easily to her. Sarah Elbert in *A Hunger for Home: Louisa May Alcott and "Little Women,"* concluded, "Jo's journey is the only fully complete one in *Little Women* and it involves her learning to tell true love from romantic fancy." Elbert added that while the girls are ultimately paired up with men they truly love, Jo's marriage comes closest to Alcott's ideal, largely because Jo is closest to Alcott's ideal woman.

At first, the marriage of Laurie to Amy seems odd, but Alcott shows how well-matched they are for each other. They both have fine tastes and prefer a lifestyle of luxury to hard work. Further, Amy likes to be taken care of, something Jo would never allow Laurie to do for her.

Style

Point of View

Little Women is written from a third-person omniscient perspective. The narrator knows the girls' personalities, thoughts, and feelings intimately. This allows the reader to see happenings that the family often does not, such as when Jo cries because she is secretly disappointed that Amy is the one going to Europe.

The narrator also knows the girls' futures, as there are occasional references to what will happen at a future time. Alcott uses both subtle foreshadowing and explicit references to future events. When the Marches and the Laurences set up their makeshift post office, the Laurence's gardener sends a secret love letter to Hannah, the March's housekeeper. Alcott comments, "How they laughed when the secret came out, never dreaming how many love letters that little post office would hold in the years to come!" This statement not only intrigues adolescent readers, but also foreshadows future pleasant letters as well as the cruel joke Laurie plays on Meg by sending forged love letters.

The omniscient narrator does not abuse her power by censoring the characters' faults and mishaps. On the contrary, flaws and bad judgment are included in the story to add a dimension of realism and make the characters believable. Laurie's cruel joke on Meg, Meg's silly domestic dramas as a wife, Jo's intentionally not telling Amy to be careful on the ice—all of these show the characters as human beings with faults.

Structure

The structure of *Little Women* is episodic, alternating stories of each of the sisters. Each chapter focuses primarily on an incident in one of the girls' lives. This structure accomplishes two things. First, it requires a relatively short attention span that is appropriate for Alcott's young audience. Second, this structure makes it easier to see the girls' growth as young women. Rather than charting subtle cues, as an author might in an adult novel, Alcott allows the reader to see changes in the characters each time they are revisited. For example, at the beginning of the novel, Jo is unconcerned with her appearance and keeps her hair down, her clothes crumpled, and her boots untied. In subsequent scenes, Jo is seen tying her boots and putting her hair up, so that the reader notices the changes easily. Readers become aware that while they were watching Meg, Beth, and Amy, Jo grew up a little. The same is true for the other sisters, too.

Domestic-Centered Settings

Given the novel's time period and cast of characters, it is no surprise that the book is filled with domestic concerns and activities. Alcott takes this focus further, however, with her attention to detail and her settings. She is frequently commended for the amount of detail in the story with regard to clothing, manners, appearance, sewing, and entertaining. The critic Madeleine B. Stern commented that Alcott's accomplishment is in presenting universal themes brought to life by domestic details and "local flavor." She adds, "By its documentary value alone, *Little Women*, as an index of New England manners in the mid-century, would be accorded a place in literary history."

Most of the action in the story takes place in the March home. When family members travel, as when Amy goes to Europe, news of the trip is related through letters sent home. When scenes unfold somewhere other than the March home, they are generally in a nearby house (such as Laurie's or Annie Moffat's) or some other domestic setting like the outdoor picnic Laurie hosts. Confining the settings in this way serves to keep the reader's attention on the household as the girls' lives unfold in familiar surroundings.

Foreshadowing

Throughout the novel, Alcott uses foreshadowing to suggest to her readers what lies ahead. Foreshadowing is a technique that establishes the narrator's credibility and creates an air of suspense that compels the reader to keep reading. At the end of part one, Jo bemoans the fact that Meg will marry Mr. Brooke and leave home. Laurie tries to console her by saying that they will have great fun after Meg is gone, and that they will go on a trip abroad to lift Jo's spirits. Jo only responds that Laurie's plan is nice, but "there's no knowing what may happen in three years." Three years later, Meg marries, and, shortly after, Laurie graduates from college and proposes to Jo. When she rejects him, he is devastated and goes abroad without her.

Beth's death is foreshadowed on at least three occasions. Early in the novel, in chapter 4, Alcott writes:

> There are many Beths in the world, shy and quiet, sitting in corners till needed, and living for others so cheerfully that no one sees the sacrifices till the little cricket on the hearth stops chirping, and the sweet, sunshiny presence vanishes, leaving silence and shadow behind.

This passage foreshadows Beth's untimely death and the deep grief felt by her family at her passing. Later, as Jo considers whether or not to overhaul her novel manuscript for publication, Beth says only that she wants to see the book printed soon, and there is something in the way Beth says "soon" that propels Jo into action. Finally, as Amy prepares to leave for Europe, she tearfully hugs Laurie good-bye as she asks him to look after the family. He promises to do so and says that if anything should happen, he will come and comfort her. Alcott adds that he promises this "little dreaming that he would be called upon to keep his word." In fact, Beth dies shortly thereafter. She is able to see Jo's book in print, and her death comes while both Laurie and Amy are in Europe. He finds her and comforts her, after which they fall in love and marry.

The Role of Women in Nineteenth-Century America

In the nineteenth century, women were responsible for creating warm, happy homes for their husbands and children. While some families hired servants, most could not afford to hire help. The duties of running a household were staggering. A woman prepared three rather elaborate meals every day. Housecleaning, laundry, mending, and ironing were all done with painstaking care. Daughters were expected to help with housework to expedite chores and also to learn skills for their own future households.

Women were also accountable for the actions of the family outside the home. If a man took up excessive drinking or gambling, for example, his wife was blamed for not creating a suitable home environment. To create an ideal home, the wife handled all housework in addition to being polite, selfless, virtuous, and loving.

Compare & Contrast

- **1860s:** Children's books generally depict innocent, flawless children in innocent stories. Characters are one-dimensional and stories are strongly oriented toward teaching virtue.

Today: The Newbery Medal is awarded to Christopher Paul Curtis' *Bud, Not Buddy*, a story about a ten-year-old boy who runs away from his foster home in search of his father. One of the Caldecott Honor Books is Audrey Couloumbis' *Getting Near to Baby*, which tells the story of two sisters dealing with the death of their baby sister. Another Caldecott Honor Book is Molly Bang's *When Sophie Gets Angry—Really, Really Angry*, a story about a little girl's temper tantrum.

- **1860s:** Scarlet fever, which typically afflicts children between the ages of two and ten, is of ten fatal, as treatments are terribly inadequate. Even when children survive, they often suffer poor health for years.

  Today: Since the discovery of penicillin, scarlet fever rarely claims lives. In fact, patients treated for the disease rarely even suffer lingering problems. In addition, scarlet fever is not as severe as it once was, either because the strain has weakened or because people have become more resistant to the disease.

- **Early 1860s:** The best-selling fiction books are Charles Dickens' *Great Expectations* and *Little Dorrit*, Wilkie Collins' *The Woman in White*, Mrs. Henry Woods' *East Lynne*, and Mary E. Braddon's *Lady Audley's Secret*. They are stories of crime with plots featuring bigamy, incest, and apparitions.

Today: The best-selling fiction books include J. K. Rowling's Harry Potter series, John Gr-isham's *The Testament* and *The Brethren*, Sea-mus Heaney's translation of the classic *Beowulf*, Isabel Allende's *Daughter of Fortune*, and Arthur S. Golden's *Memoirs of a Geisha*. These wide-ranging stories feature wizard apprenticeship, deception in a federal prison, adventure and romance, and coming of age in pre-World War II Japan.

- **1860s:** Young women are expected to learn cooking, sewing, laundering, and parenting. In addition, proper young ladies are well-mannered, graceful, polite, and soft-spoken. Although many women work in "men's" jobs during the Civil War, they return to their places at home once the men return from war.

Today: Women occupy virtually every career field available. They are doctors, judges, astronauts, scientists, writers, legislators, engineers, and more. At the same time, they have the option of choosing to stay home and take care of the home and rear children. Although there are lingering social norms about what constitutes ladylike behavior, millions of women have little regard for such social restrictions.

Despite the heavy domestic demands placed on a woman, it was sometimes necessary for her to seek additional work for economic reasons. While many tried to take work they could perform at home, such as laundry or sewing, others worked as governesses, teachers, or companions to the elderly. In some cases, women were able to make a living in the creative arts, such as writing. This was quite challenging because women were assumed to be inferior to men, and proper women were not expected to know very much about the outside world.

Philosophical and Social Reforms

Little Women opens during the Civil War, which took place from 1861 to 1865. Prior to that event, New England experienced a rise in philosophical interest and the spread of reform-minded-ness. The Transcendental Movement was underway, especially in Massachusetts, where Ralph Waldo Emerson and Henry David Thoreau lived. Transcendentalism rejected Puritanism, religious dogma, and strict adherence to rituals. Instead, it embraced individualism and naturalism, maintaining that there is a deep connection between the universe and the human soul. American transcendentalism officially began in 1836 in Boston, with the formation of the Transcendental Club, whose members included Emerson, Thoreau, Margaret Fuller, and Bronson Alcott.

Early in the nineteenth century, middle-class women began joining evangelical societies that promoted social and moral reform. As conflict mounted over the issue of slavery, women became involved, and by 1850 most members of abolitionist groups were women. From these beginnings sprang the women's rights movement, which would steadily gain momentum well into the twentieth century.

Education

Nineteenth-century formal education in America was limited, as evidenced by the fact that in 1860 there were only a hundred public high schools. Although there were more elementary schools, only about half of all children attended, and then only for forty-five days per year. Children were taught reading, writing, spelling, and arithmetic, and sometimes history, geography, and grammar. Learning took the form of memorization and recitation, as opposed to critical thinking or creativity. This approach contrasts to Bronson Alcott's teaching methods, which were designed to encourage his daughters to think for themselves and learn facts instead of memorizing them for the short term.

Louisa certainly understood the distinction between her educational experience and that of many of her peers. Many families who were dissatisfied with public schooling opted to teach their children at home. Those who could afford it hired tutors for their children, as represented in the novel by Laurie's tutor, John Brooke. Formal education generally ended when a student turned fourteen or fifteen, especially when the student was female.

Discipline in public school was often harsh and humiliating. Corporal punishment, such as spanking or swatting, was common, although not all parents agreed with these methods. In *Little Women*, Amy is subjected to this sort of treatment by her teacher when she is caught with limes at school. Her teacher swats her hands and forces her to stand in front of the class until recess. Mrs. March agrees not to send Amy back to school, so she pursues her studies at home with Beth.

The Civil War

When the Civil War ended, more than 600,000

men had lost their lives and others were disabled. More Americans died in the Civil War than in all other American wars combined from the colonial period through the Vietnam War. It is unknown how many civilians were killed by guerrillas, deserters, and soldiers.

Because so many men were killed or seriously wounded in the war, American families were faced with the difficult task of supporting themselves without the help of the man of the house. Meager pensions to widows and veterans were not enough to restore financial stability. To make matters worse, most men were forever changed by the experience. Most had never traveled beyond their home towns, and serving in the military took them far away where they faced loneliness, fear, and daily confrontation with death and suffering. As veterans, they assembled in organizations and fostered a sense of patriotism for their sacrifices. For African Americans, serving in the military was beneficial in its own way because they could then make strong cases for citizenship.

During the war, women assumed larger roles in the social structure. They became temporary nurses, clerks, and factory workers. A few hundred women even disguised themselves as soldiers and fought on the battlefields. Once the war was over, however, traditional roles were resumed.

The economic consequences of the war were formidable. Consider that in 1860, the federal budget was $63 million, and by 1879, the total expenditures for the war were calculated at over $6 billion. This created extreme debt and limited the government's ability to function as it had prior to the war. In the South, economic hardship became the norm. Railroads, industrial operations, mechanical equipment, and livestock had been spent or destroyed. In contrast, the economy in the North thrived during and after the war. Statistics show that between 1860 and 1870, Northern wealth increased by 50 percent, while Southern wealth decreased by 60 percent. The Reconstruction Period, which represented efforts to reunite the country in political, economic, and social terms, would last twelve years—triple the length of the war.

Critical Overview

Although Louisa May Alcott wrote *Little Women* in 1868 for the sole purpose of making money, the novel is without question her most notable and enduring work. In fact, the book as it is read today contains the original text and its sequel, *Good Wives*, which was written a year after the first part. The second part was written in response to the demands of Alcott's young female readers, who were drawn to the individuality displayed by the novel's characters and wanted to know what would become of them. Upon the April 14 release of part two, Alcott's publisher was shocked by its sales. By the end of May, more than 13,000 copies had sold —an incredible number at the time, and especially surprising because the book was written for young girls, not the general public. Critical response in 1868 and 1869 was as favorable as the readers' response, and Alcott was among the first children's authors to be taken seriously by literary critics. A review in *Nation* declared *Little Women* an "agreeable" story that appeals to juvenile and adult readers alike. The critic wrote that the March girls were "drawn with a certain cleverness."

When the second part of the novel was published, a critic wrote in *Harper's New Monthly Magazine* that it was perhaps too mature for adolescent girls, but that it rings true by not resorting to the "false sentiment" so common in children's literature. In fact, Alcott's contemporaries as well as modernday critics agree that the novel is remarkable for its reality and depth, standing in stark contrast to the too-sweet, overly didactic stories available to children at the time. Children were generally depicted as perfect and innocent, but Alcott gave her characters flaws and made no effort to conceal them. They remain virtuous, however, because they are aware of their weaknesses and strive to correct them. In modern terms, the characters in *Little Women* seem a bit too perfect, as many critics argue, but in the context of the mid-nineteenth century, they were characters whose likeness had never been seen. Not all critics praise the novel, however. Biographer Martha Saxton viewed *Little Women* as a sell-out for Alcott, who, according to Saxton, had great talent, yet squandered it on a book that was preachy and sentimental. Jane Gabin in *Reference Guide to American Literature*, on the other hand, deemed *Little Women* "markedly superior to other books of its genre" because of its unobtrusive "sermonizing" and its well-rounded characters. She added that in other books of the time, the villains and the heroes were clearly identified, but in Alcott's book, even the heroes have flaws and make mistakes. Lavinia Russ of *Horn Book* had a different view on the appeal of the book, arguing that the story teaches that life does not always provide neatly bundled happy endings, but that girls should still strive to be good people.

Alcott's sense of the challenges and joys of adolescence continues to impress readers. Since its publication, *Little Women* has never gone out of print, and some scholars attribute its staggering success to the universal themes of growing up and to Alcott's honest portrayal of the feelings, thoughts, worries, and delights that accompany it. In *New England Quarterly*, Madeleine Stern observed:

> The author's knowledge of adolescent psychology reveals itself in twofold form throughout the work, for it consisted first of an appeal to adolescents, the skill of making them laugh or cry, and secondly of an ability to describe adolescents, to catch and transfix the varied emotions and thoughts of the young.

Feminist critics are divided about the portrayal of females in *Little Women*. While some criticize the heavily domestic depiction of womanhood, others praise Jo as a breakout figure who blazes her own path and is able to have both love and a career. The fact that, in part two, Jo marries a man who is older and lacks passion seems too great a compromise to some critics who admired Jo's steadfast adherence to her principles in part one. Further, they interpret her working at Plumfield with her husband as sacrificing her writing after marriage.

Although the book is filled with submissive women who are content with domestic life (such as Meg), a great deal of feminist attention concentrates on Jo. Brigid Brophy of *New York Times Book Review* agreed that while the book is heavily sentimental, it still works because of the extraordinary character of Jo. Less taken with the novel, Elizabeth Janeway in *Only Connect: Readings on Children's Literature,* described it as "dated and sentimental and full of preaching and moralizing," but admitted that Jo makes the book worth reading nonetheless. She wrote that "Jo is ... the one young woman in nineteenth-century fiction who maintains her individual independence, who gives up no part of her autonomy as payment for being a woman." Alison Lurie of *New York Review of Books* seems to agree with this notion, as she commented:

> From a mid-nineteenth century perspective, *Little Women* is both a conservative and a radical novel.... In contemporary terms, [Jo] has it all: Not only a household and children but two careers and she doesn't have to do her own housework and cooking.

Critics continue to debate the lasting qualities of *Little Women.* Whether it is the novel's touching presentation of growing pains, the triumphant female figure Jo, or the overall "human truth," as British author and critic G. K. Chesterton claims, there is no doubt that the novel as a whole has an enduring appeal. Despite its setting in a time and place unfamiliar to modern readers, the novel continues to speak to children and adults in a way that transcends mere nostalgia.

Sources

Brophy, Brigid, "A Masterpiece, and Dreadful," in *New York Times Book Review*, January 17, 1965, pp. 1, 44.

Chesterton, G. K., "Louisa Alcott," in *A Handful of Authors: Essays on Books and Writers*, Sheed and Ward, 1953, pp. 163-67.

Elbert, Sarah, *A Hunger for Home: Louisa May Alcott and "Little Women,"* Temple University Press, 1984.

Gabin, Jane S., "*Little Women:* Overview," in *Reference Guide to American Literature*, 3rd edition, St. James Press, 1994.

Janeway, Elizabeth, "Meg, Jo, Beth, Amy, and Louisa," in *Only Connect: Readings on Children's Literature*, edited by Sheila Egoff, G. T. Stubbs, and L. F. Ashley, Oxford University Press, 1969, pp. 286, 288, 290.

Lurie, Alison, "She Had It All," in *New York Review of Books*, March 2, 1995, pp. 3-5.

Moss, Joyce, and George Wilson, eds., *Literature and Its Times: Profiles of 300 Notable Literary Works and the Historical Events That Influenced Them*, Vol. 2: *Civil Wars to Frontier Societies (1800–1880s)*, The Gale Group, 1997.

Review of *Little Women*, in *Harper's New Monthly Magazine*, Vol. 39, August 1869, pp. 455-56.

Review of *Little Women*, in *Nation*, Vol. 7, No. 173, October 22, 1868, p. 335.

Russ, Lavinia, "Not To Be Read on Sunday," in *Horn Book*, October 1968, pp. 524, 526.

Saxton, Martha, *Louisa May: A Modern Biography of Louisa May Alcott*, Houghton Mifflin, 1977.

Showalter, Elaine, *Sister's Choice: Tradition and Change in American Women's Writing*, Clarendon Press (Oxford), 1991, pp. 42-64.

Stern, Madeleine B., "Louisa May Alcott: An Appraisal," in *New England Quarterly*, Vol. 22, No. 4, December 1949, pp. 475-98.

For Further Study

Cogan, Frances B., *All American Girls: The Ideal of Real Womanhood in Mid-Nineteenth Century America*, University of Georgia Press, 1989.

> Cogan presents a historical perspective on women's roles in mid-nineteenth century America, including their expected educational levels, skills, aspirations, and manners. She suggests that in addition to the traditional view of womanhood, there was a competing view of a more dynamic, independent type of woman emerging in literature.

Fetterley, Judith, "*Little Women:* Alcott's Civil War," in *Feminist Studies*, Vol. 5, No. 2, Summer 1979, pp. 369-83.

> Fetterley proposes that Alcott's text reflects compromises in style and content that came about as the result of the demands placed on the author by her publisher and her public.

Jefferson, Margo, "Books of the Times: *Little Women*, Growing Up Then and Now," in *New York Times*, December 21, 1994.

> Jefferson describes the March household as being as divided as its

author, and relates the classic novel to Gerald Earley's *Daughters: On Family and Fatherhood.*

Meyerson, Joel, and Madeleine B. Stern, eds., *The Selected Letters of Louisa May Alcott: A Life of the Creator of "Little Women,"* University of Georgia Press, 1995.

This collection of Alcott's correspondence gives insight into her domestic life, her thoughts, and her personality apart from her success as a children's writer.

Stern, Madeleine B., ed., *Behind a Mask: The Unknown Thrillers of Louisa May Alcott*, William Morrow, 1997.

These frightening, passionate, and suspenseful tales reveal the other side of Alcott's writing, which she preferred to her better-known children's stories.